The Lady who was Beautiful Inside

for Victoria

07 08 09 10 11 SDB 10 9 8 7 6 5 4 3 2 1

ISBN-13: 978-0-7407-6866-8
ISBN-10: 0-7407-6866-2

www.edwardmonkton.com

www.andrewsmcmeel.com

ATTENTION: SCHOOLS AND BUSINESSES

Andrews McMeel books are available at quantity discounts with bulk purchase for educational, business, or sales promotional use. For information, please write to: Special Sales Department, Andrews McMeel Publishing, LLC, 4520 Main Street, Kansas City, Missouri 64111.

The LADY who was BEAUTIFUL INSIDE

Edward Monkton

Andrews McMeel Publishing, LLC

Kansas City

There was once
a LADY.

One day when she
was sitting at the
HAIRDRESSER
She picked up a
magazine.

"Oh, hairdresser," she said.
"Look at all these BEAUTIFUL
ladies. See how their LEGS
reach up to the sky. See
how their BOSOMS are
firm and perfect.

"See how every GLOSSY hair lies perfectly in place. And see how they have no sign of CROW'S-FEET EYES or ORANGE-PEEL BOTTOM.

"Why do I BOTHER, hairdresser? Why? Why? WHY?"

And she held the leg of the hairdresser and began to SOB noiselessly into his trousers.

"Lady," said the hairdresser, "do not DESPAIR. Look at your SMILE."

The lady LOOKED.

"Nobody has a smile as BEAUTIFUL as you," said the hairdresser. "Not even the ladies in the magazines. And that, lady, is because your beauty comes from DEEP WITHIN you. And that is the most beautiful BEAUTY of all."

"Oh, hairdresser," said the lady, "do you think so? Do you REALLY think so?"

"I KNOW so," said the hairdresser. "Just take a walk outside and you will see."

At that, the hairdresser VANISHED and the lady walked out of the salon into the rain.

As she SMILED, an amazing thing happened. The rain stopped and the SUN broke through the clouds.

Flowers BLOOMED in her footsteps, birds began to SING and the trees burst into BLOSSOM.

The people in the street
began to CHEER and
little children DANCED
all around her in a circle,
LAUGHING.

"Well I never!" exclaimed the lady, a little flustered. "Oh goodness gracious me!

"Could it be that the hairdresser was RIGHT or is this just a STRANGE and FORTUNATE coincidence?"

In the end it did not matter. For the lady had seen the POWER of the beauty INSIDE her.

And from then on, everywhere she went, LOVELINESS happened.

For she did have a very BEAUTIFUL beauty indeed.

THE END